WALKING FOOT QUILTING

FOR BEGINNERS

A Fresh Guide To Quilt Using The Walking Foot.
Special Techniques And Tips On Using The Feed Dog,
Guide Bar And The Walking Foot As You start Quilting

By

Rebecca Halley

WALKING FOOT QUILTING FOR BEGINNERS

A Fresh Guide To Quilt Using The Walking Foot. Special Techniques And Tips On Using The Feed Dog, Guide Bar And The Walking Foot As You start Quilting

By

Rebecca Halley

Table Of Content

Acknowledgement

Quilting is fun, and a book about walking foot which has made quilting a lot easier is necessary. I would like to admit that this book wouldn't have been possible without help and support I received from different individuals and groups.

I thank my editors, my research partners, cover designer and all who have contributed in one way or the other for the success of this book. I also thank my family members, friends and well wishers for moral support and encouragement especially when things seem really tough for me.

Also, I cannot forget you reading this book now. Without your purchase and support, this book will be gathering dust, and it would greatly discourage me. I thank you for picking a copy, and I do hope that all you want to know about the walking foot is embedded here in this book. Thank you!

Introduction

Quilting becomes easier and more captivating when important add-ons and accessories like the walking foot are introduced. Back in the days, it would be difficult to come across any quilting books. However, with lots of advancement in the quilting filed, quilters now enjoy the vast collection of books, guides, magazines and blogs on quilting.

This book is intended for those who are new to quilting with the walking foot. It covers all you need to know about the walking foot, explains the parts of the walking foot, and also the different types. It doesn't just stop there. In this book, you will also learn about how to quilt with the walking foot and various helpful hints and tips to make your quilting perfect, even though this is your first time of quilting with the walking foot. There are some troubles you might face while using the walking foot, and this book does justice by addressing these issues.

There are many other quitting tips and fresh ideas you will learn from this book. You will learn about the guide bar and how to install it. As you sincerely search deep for valuable resources to help you become a professional quilter, I do hope that this book adds hugely to your knowledge not only about the walking foot, but quilting in general.

Chapter I

Walking Foot Exposed

What The Heck Is A Walking Foot?

At first, after hearing the phrase *"walking foot"* what comes to your mind? Sincerely speaking, I thought of it in a literal sense. Yes, I thought it meant the foot we used for walking. Was I wrong?

Actually, I wasn't wrong if judged by the literal sense of the phrase. However, when it comes to quilting, I would certainly be mocked and laughed at by quilters, especially those advanced in the field. So, let's take a look at walking foot and its important details.

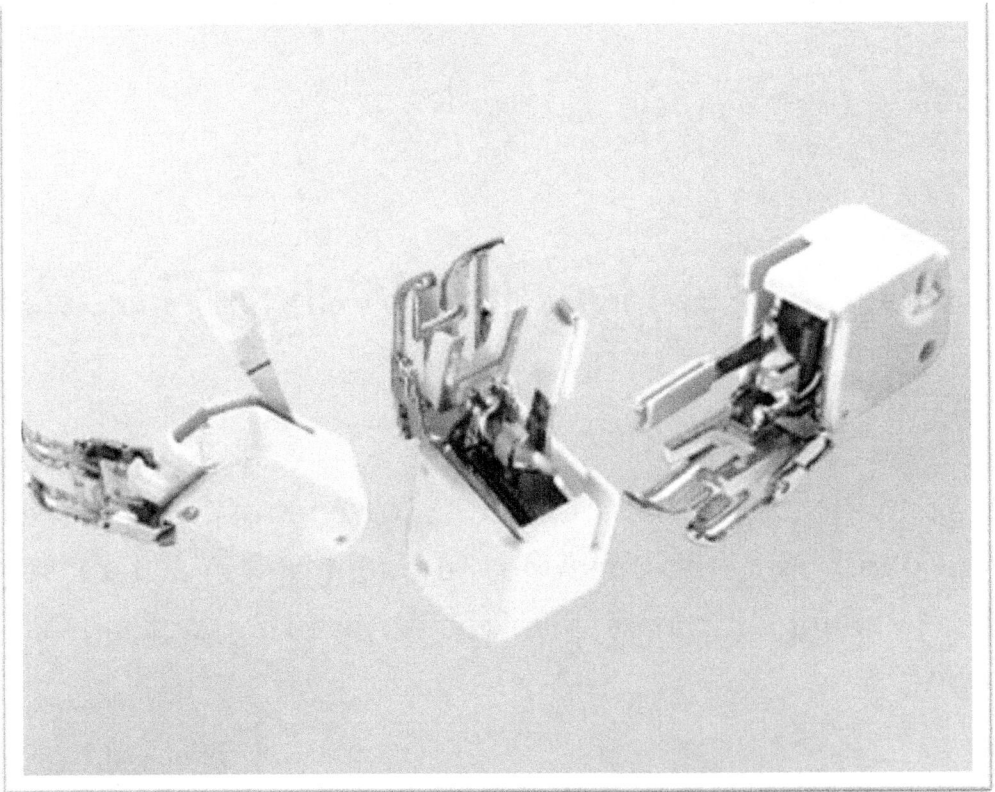

The Walking Foot As Shown From Various Angles

Vital details about the walking foot.

When it comes to quilting, you have to choose one of these methods:

1. Walking foot quilting.
2. Free motion quilting.

Those new to the sewing world might have been hearing about the "walking foot" and wondered what it is. The main purpose of a walking foot is to prevent the bottom layer of the quilt from getting pulled through. Not just that, it keeps the top from lagging behind.

The walking foot does something similar like the feed dog. It helps pulls the piece of clothing through on the bottom, and at the same time pulls the top layer. This is done with a perfect timing, ensuring that the bottom and the top too gets to squeeze all fabric layers, and still the same magnitude of force is used in pulling them through.

If you have ever tried to quilt using a minky backing, then you must agree with me that it isn't easy. Try a walking foot, then you will be surprised at how easy things get and it makes your quilting flow! Another awesome fact I love the walking foot it that it makes sewing multiple layers super easy!

Also known as an even-feed foot and even a dual feed foot, it is designed to making quilting easier and also uniformly feed the several quilt layers through your machine. Designed with unique teeth at the bottom, the walking foot can easily get hold of the quilt surface. With this, the quick movement made by your feed dogs is easily copied.

With the help of a walking foot, there won't be any folding or bunching because it is designed to ensure that all layers smoothly fall under the needle when quilting. It also ensures that you get a consistent size of stitches. All the tough work is done for you by the foot!

Superb Things You Can Do With Your Walking Foot

At this point you should begin to see the walking foot as a huge presser foot which makes your sewing machine stand out. With this little equipment, you get an added advantage as you sew. Your sewing machine now seems to have super powers since the walking foot provides it with an added set of feed dogs to be utilized for the top part of the fabric you are sewing.

This makes it super easy for you to manage certain complex types of fabrics. Matching plaids becomes easy to sew. Knits easily flow through your machine without pilling up. Even those thick layers of multiple folds in massive projects won't be troublesome to sew.

Majorly, the walking foot is used for:

1. Plaid matching

   The walking foot is a great add-on when it comes to matching stripes, plaids and other similar types of prints. If you are planning to sew a material which has a defined pattern or even directional prints and this fabric needs to be professionally matched across major seams, then a walking foot will do the magic. In this case, the walking foot will act nicely to ensure that that these pieces of fabric easily move through as you sew without shifting an inch.

2. Sewing heavy materials

   Fabrics that are thick and heavy in nature makes sewing difficult. However, with the help of a walking foot, you can easily sew upholstery fabric, heavy wool and even several layers of terrycloth, just to mention a few.

3. Machine quilting

   When it comes to stitch in the ditch (machine quilting), the walking foot is of tremendous help. As you quilt, the walking foot helps in keeping the fabric and the batting layers together. It is very handy when you are using machine to quilt large gently curved lines and straight line too.

4. Slippery materials

Sometimes when you are sewing slippery materials, you are forced to pin up excessively to hold the fabric in place. You don't need this anymore with the walking foot! Yes, you heard that right. Satin and other slippery materials are damaged easily when you use pins on them. With the walking foot, you get to eliminate the need of these pins and still sew your slippery fabric perfectly!

5. Sewing knit fabrics

One of the characteristics of knit fabrics is that they are stretchy in nature. This is good in other aspects; however, it is bad for sewing. As you sew, you want everything to come out perfect without squeezing. Well, the knit fabric won't come out as you expect. Such material would usually get stretched out as you sew under the presser foot. This mostly happens when you sew in the same direction of the stretch like sewing on the edge of your T-shirt. It also happens when you sew with a fabric that is highly stretchy in nature like a rib knit. The consoling news is that your walking foot holds everything in the right place and moves the knit materials in an even manner to prevent them from stretching out of shape.

6. Sewing plastics and leather

When sewing sticky materials, you could find it difficult since it is hard for the presser foot to glide over the surface. This is where the walking foot comes to the rescue. Designed in such a way to make feeding material under the needle easy, the walking foot is ideal for sewing plastic, leather, oilcloth, vinyl and other related materials.

7. Topstitching binding

Sometimes, after topstitching, you get to notice strange drag lines within your button placket or hem. For some, a quick fix would be applying steam. However, this doesn't always settle the issue because even after a blast of steam, these strange drag lines would still be there.

Even if you carefully press the fabric before you begin, a folded and topstitched layer of fabric could still appear messy. This is because your normal presser foot might feed the top layer at an increased speed compared to the layer at the bottom.

This is highly likely when stitch is very far away from the edge you folded, like on a very deep hem. All these issues shouldn't cause you worries when you use the walking foot. It greatly assists in keeping all the layers even to provide an end result of sweet edges that are pleasing to the eyes.

What You Can't Do With The Walking Foot

We have been taking about how perfect the walking foot can make your quilting become and the numerous advantage of this magical tool. Sadly, the walking foot has its own limitations. Always remember not to use the walking foot in the following situations:

- **Reverse sewing**
  Unfortunately, you can't use your walking foot in reverse. The top feed dogs of your walking foot are designed to make your fabric move forward. The machine feed dogs are there to move your material backward.

- **Broad Pretty Stitches**
  If you plan on doing wide decorative stitches, then be prepared to engage in some side to side fabric movement. This is a task the walking foot isn't designed to perform.

- **Free-motion quilting**

  Since your walking foot is designed to aid the fabric from slipping and also to move forward, you can't use it in free-motion quilting where you can move your fabric side to side.

Limitations of the walking foot

As magical and useful as the walking foot is, there are certain limits it can't cross. So, before you start using it, you need to first of all know the limitations and the areas it can't go beyond. With that said, limitations of the walking foot include:

1. **Design limitations and movement range:** With your walking foot, it is very easy to make straight lines that appear perfectly. You can also make lines that are curved gently with your walking foot. However, when it comes to complex designs, it would be very difficult to use your walking foot for such. The best approach for such complex designs is the free motion quilting.

The other one is:

2. **The direction:** The walking foot is designed in such a way that depends on the directional feed dog of your machine. Because of this, you can only use it for quilting

in two (2) directions. One is the straightforward direction, while the other one is in reverse.

What this implies is that as you quilt, you adjust the quilt to ensure that the walking foot is moving forward along the path you intend using. As you quilt with the walking foot, when it is time to change directions, you will have to make the necessary rotations and adjustments until it faces the proper direction. This can be tedious, however, with time, you'll get used to it.

One thing to note is that you shouldn't just go ahead to shift and also rotate your quilt. Before this is done, ensure that you position your needle downwards. This will help keep your quilt at the proper position without shifting it out of place.

Explaining The Parts Of The Walking Foot

Also called a "plaid matcher," the dual-feed of the walking foot assists in keeping plaids, stripes and any other shape that is geometric in nature lined up in a perfect sense. This is because of the little but special parts it is made of.

When you get hold of the walking foot, you might begin to wonder what those little metal parts do and how they operate. The great news here is that it doesn't bite! (Just kidding).

Generally, the walking foot consists of three (3) major parts which are:

1. The arm
2. The sole
3. The upper feed dogs

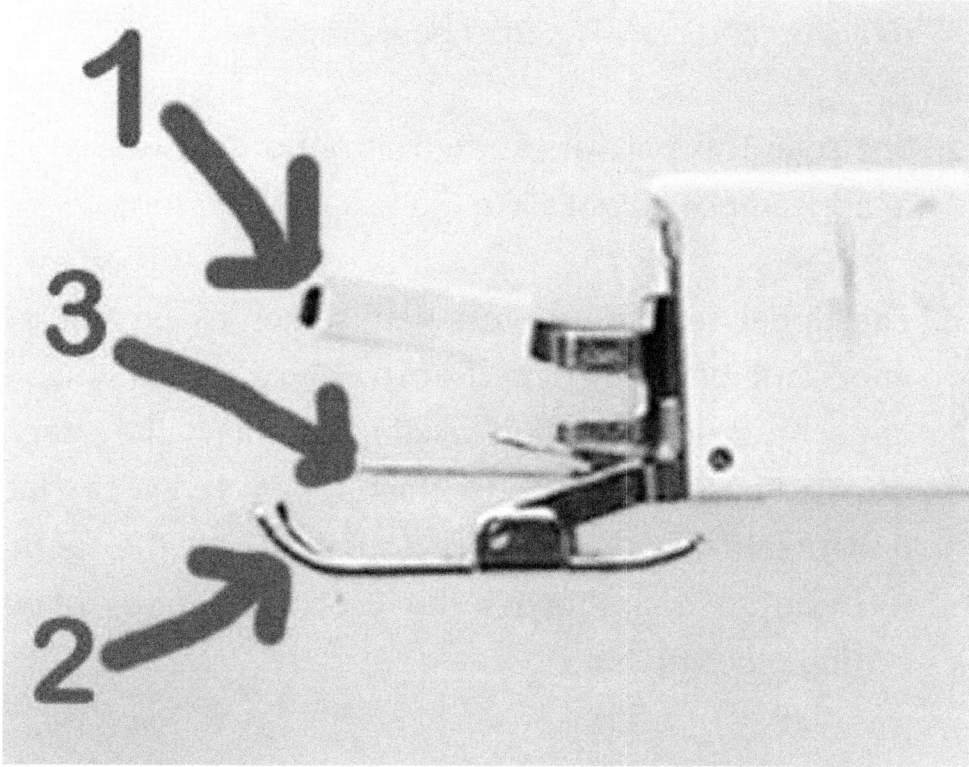

Walking Foot Showing The Main Parts

1. **The arm:** This part of the walking foot simply sits and fits on the screw which is used in firmly holding the needle of the machine in place. This makes it possible for it to move up and down as the needle moves.

2. **The sole:** This part sits at the bottom of the walking foot. In appearance, it looks like the usual zigzag foot.

3. **The upper feed dogs:** this part seems to be the most important because it performs a very crucial role. The upper feed dogs of your walking foot plays the vital role of feeding (or walking) the upper layer of fabric underneath the presser foot together with the fabric at the bottom that touches the usual feed dogs of your sewing machine.

When the material you are sewing is finding it difficult to get underneath the presser foot, this comes handy. Due to how high they are, you could face a difficult time trying to sew bulky fabrics as they don't easily flow underneath the presser foot. This is one of the problems they upper feed dogs solve, helping these bulky fabrics flow properly. Such material could be bulky fabrics like various jean layers or even felted wool sweaters.

Before You Buy A Walking Foot

It is important to note that even though the walking foot is an awesome sewing accessory, you should consider purchasing one that is compatible with your machine, a walking foot you can install and remove easily.

Though small in size, the walking foot is a machine on its own.

How To Install A Walking Foot

Installing a walking foot on your machine could seem tricky at first, but with time, everything gets to seem very easy. The very first thing to note is the type of machine you are using. Since all machines are not the same, installing a walking foot could seem a bit different on various machines. Nevertheless, here are the steps of installing your walking foot:

Step one: The first thing here is to carefully detach the regular sewing foot that comes with your machine. For some, it could be as easy as snapping off the foot extension that is interchangeable; for other machines, you have to unscrew the foot, then remove everything.

If you machine requires unscrewing, then you should first of all raise the presser foot. It is also advisable to bring the needle out to make things easier, especially if this is your first time of installing a walking foot.

Step two: After detaching the regular sewing foot, the foot should be lowered, then you carefully mount the walking foot in position. Note that lowering the foot won't be necessary as time goes by because you must have mastered how to fit-in the walking foot. Lowering the foot only makes in very easy for you now as a beginner.

As you put the walking foot in place, take note of the clamp on the walking foot. This sets in place over the screw hole. The arm of the walking foot is designed to align with the needle clamp/screw. The feed dogs too are lowered due to the lowered needle.

Step Three: Insert the screw, then firmly tighten it so that the walking foot stays fit.

Step four: Now, you should raise up the foot. After that, insert the needle and also thread the needle. With that done, pull out the thread through to the back/left of your presser foot, and the feeds dogs should get raised together with the needle.

That's it, all set!

Which Version Of The Walking Foot Should You Choose?

Generally, there are two versions of the walking foot out there, namely:

1. The classic version
2. Open toe version

1. **The classic version:**
   This version of the walking foot has been around for a long time. It provides all the benefits you get with the walking foot. This version is designed to provide a better support to your fabric as you push the needle through it. You should pick this classic version when you don't need an added visibility of the sewing area. Generally, it is cheaper compared to the open toe version.

2. **The open toe version:**
   The major advantage of this open toe walking foot is that it offers that extra visibility and added marks too. It is

best used for machine quilting and binding. If you use a machine to quilt and do a lot of "stitch in the ditch" this open toe version is ideal. This is because it gives you that space and freedom to see the exact points where the needle lands on the fabric as you quilt.

Chapter II

Be On Guard With The Guide Bars

Guide bars are important as you use your walking foot to quilt. They don't just provide support, but also makes the walking foot perform superbly and exceptionally.

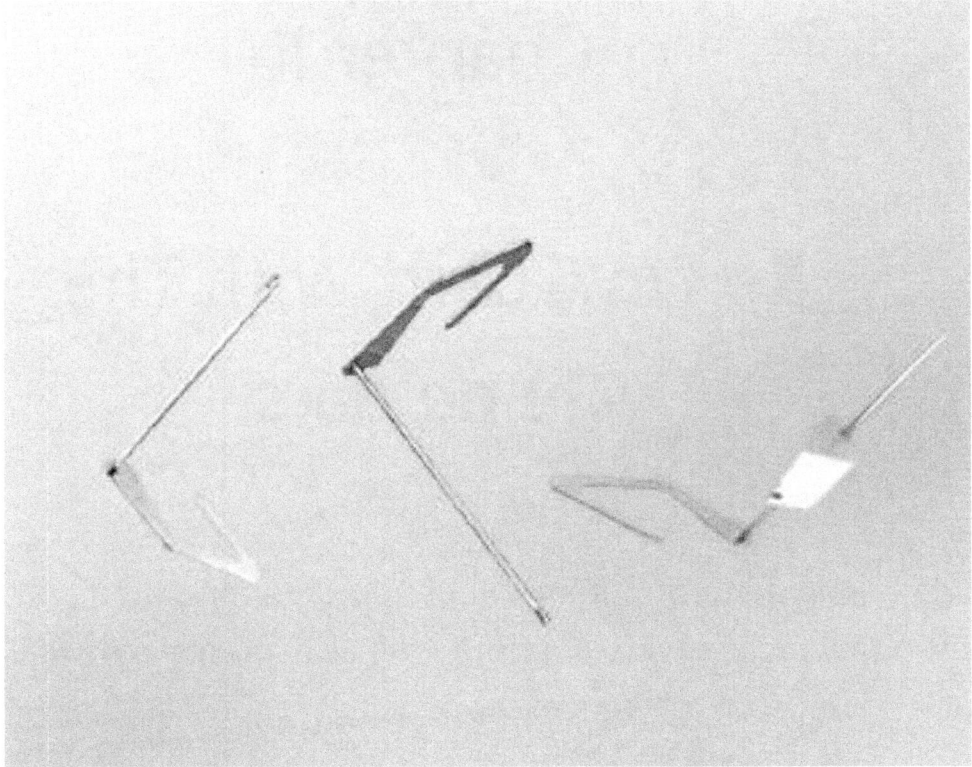

Guide Bars Shown At Different Angles

Importance Of Guide Bars

Guide bars are really important. They are attached to the feet of the sewing machine in various ways to ensure that as you sew, you are able to repeat the stitching rows which stand far apart from the markings.

Although the foot's edge can serve as a guideline when you stitch, however, it may produce terrible results. You might get stitching lines that are very close to one another, and this could lead to dense stitching.

You might ask "what about using chalk, tapes or pins for marking the stitching lines of the fabric?" This isn't advisable and would cause troubles in the long run. As it stands, you will come across different types of guide bars suitable for your sewing machine.

Some machines are manufactured with their own guide bars which work in harmony with the walking foot holder or any foot it comes with. If this is the case, then you shouldn't bother about installing another guide bar on your sewing machine.

Guide bars help not just for quilting projects, but also are vital to ensure smooth binding. When used with the walking foot, the guide bar produces excellent result. This is mostly evident when sewing fabrics that are stretchy in nature just like knit fabrics. Because of their nature, such fabrics are prone to shifting unexpectedly when sewing, however, the guide bar and the walking foot helps keeps things in check and under control.

As you begin to use the guide bar, note that it is possible for you to create a zigzag stitch in your walking foot using the guide bar. With the guide bar attached to your walking foot, you can shift a little bit from the straight stitch. You can also use the zigzag stitch to create a patterned zigzag stitch in a forward direction.

Nevertheless, even if the guide bar can assist in creating a zigzag patterned stitch with your walking foot, you cannot use it for sewing reverse stitches with your walking foot. No matter what you attach to your walking foot, it is never possible to use it for reverse stitching. This is simply because the walking foot isn't designed for reverse stitching. If you try to force it, there is a very high possibility for your fabric to get damaged.

Various Guide Bar Types

As you dive into the world of quilting, it is necessary that you pick a guide bar that is suitable with your walking foot to make the quilting journey a memorable one. There are several types of guide bars you can choose including:

i.   **Sliding Guide Bar:**
     This type of guide bar is unique in its way because it makes it possible for you to align the previous stitched rows. You can adjust this guide bar as you want, and it can get firmly locked when you have established the distance between the stitched lines. This sliding guide bar is exceptional since it can become attached directly to the foot holder just with one soft click to lock it in place.

ii. **Border Guide Bar:**
     This is great for decorative stitches. It is recommended because it places in between the two lines that are

stitched with the decorative alternate stitch. One outstanding feature of this border guide bar is that it is designed with a transparent view, making it possible for you to check and observe where the former stitching lines have been made.

iii.   Even Feed Guide Bars

With this type of guide bar, you can support rows that have been stitched already to be aligned. The even feed guide bars are suitable for the models of sewing machine in which the white screw goes over the walking feet or even feed.

How To Attach Your Quilting Bar (Guide Bar) To Your Walking Foot

Those who have faced difficulty when they try to stitch straight lines on a huge quilt projects might have missed something vital. They might have missed the walking foot with guide bars.

Before we move ahead, what is a guide bar? The guide bar contains gridlines which assist you to sew straight in your quilting project. No matter how different they might appear, the end goal is to eliminate difficulty and help you attain the perfect finish as you quilt.

At first, the guide bar together with the walking foot on your machine might seem complex, however, it is pretty simple to make use of it. Fixing your guide bar to your walking foot shouldn't be a big deal. However, I guess this is your first time, so it is good to take things one after the other.

Attaching your guide bar involves detaching the foot already installed in your machine for sewing. Then you should concentrate on the foot holder, also called the presser foot adaptor.

You shouldn't forget to turn the wheel of your sewing machine so that the needle gets to the top, the upmost position actually. With that done, the presser foot should be raised, then stay away from the iron plate.

With this done, the walking foot can be attached, however, the guide bar should be placed in it before doing so.

Does this sound complicated? Don't worry, here's a step-by-step guide on how to attach the guide bar to the walking foot:

Step One: Detach The Standard Foot

For you to return the walking foot back to your sewing machine with the guide bar, you should take away the presser foot already on the machine. You can do this by removing the presser foot holder or by detaching the holder screw. Taking them out is important so that you will be able to access the needle and the presser bar. If you wish, you can take away the needle.

Removing the presser foot of your machine involves pushing the lever of the foot which can be found just behind the adaptors. As you do so, the presser foot will be detached. Once removed, ensure that you keep the presser foot in a secure location.

There's a set of screw on the side of the adaptor, and you can use your screwdriver to unscrew them. If you have a new sewing machine, it is advisable to be careful with the screw. Applying a bit of elbow grease is advisable and you shouldn't forcefully try to unscrew it. Using sheer force might cause damage to the thread.

Step Two: Detach The Foot Adaptor

Removing the foot adaptor is easy but should be done with care.

Step Three: Mount The Walking Foot On The Presser Foot

When you have successfully removed the presser foot and the adaptor, it is time to connect the walking foot to it. Once done, you have to raise the lever (also called the lobster claw) in order to slip over the clamp bar of the needle.

Step Four: Tighten The Foot

Now that your walking foot has been attached to the presser foot of your sewing machine, it is time to hold it firmly using the screw of your presser foot holder. This should make it firm and tight.

Step Five: Fasten The Guide Bar

With that done, you should now attach your guide bar unto your walking foot. To do so, you should place the brackets that are shaped like "U" on the top backside of your walking foot, the let all the holes be lined up.

Step Six: The Seam Guide Bar Should Be Fixed

After you must have placed the brackets, the next thing is to fix the seam guide bar onto the U-shaped bracket mounted earlier. The guide bar should be inserted straight through the walking foot, then hold it on the other side as it comes out. This process should be done again on the other part of the foot.

Step Seven: Attach The Guide Bars

Once the adjustment has been completed, the guide bars should be fixed. The guide bars should be pushed to correctly fit in, then tighten the screw located at the top back to make it firm. This will also ensure all the parts firmly fall in place. The guide bar simply falls in place and it won't need any screw set to get it tightened again.

Chapter III

Become A Walking Foot Pro With These Secrets

Tips And Trick From Beginner To Pro With Your Walking-Foot

When using the walking foot, it is important to know some useful tips and tricks which will be very helpful. The walking foot doesn't just stop at attaching the accessory and moving right ahead to quilt.

As you begin, there are some troubles and errors you might face. While some might be mild and unnoticeable, others might make you want to cry and throw your machine away because the damage would be so huge that it renders your fabric useless.

However, no need to worry because all these possible errors have been taken care of, and this chapter focuses and the tricks and secrets to make your walking foot quilting a huge success.

Achieving Straight Lines As You Quilt

Before I go on, here are some useful tips for achieving straight lines every time you sew:

1. **Always put on gloves designed for quilting**

   This might seem obvious, however, some neglect the gloves when quilting. Thin and stretchy in nature, the quilting gloves make it very easy for you to hold your fabric during the quilting process. Even if you might feel uncomfortable or there is heat, it is also a great advice to put on long sleeves as you quilt. This is because the long sleeve's fabric makes gripping your material with your elbow, and this cuts out the number of times you have to stop and start. However, you are free to ignore wearing the long sleeve if it makes you very uncomfortable, probably because the weather is too hot.

2. **Get Your Quilt Marked**

   A very important decision you can make before quilting is creating marked lines on your quilt. This is a very important step to ensure that the lines of your final stitching come out straight. You should adopt this practice even if you are not doing straight lines. This is because having a quilting plan and creating marks makes the work neat and easier.

Marking a quilt can be achieved with various methods and also different techniques. Some popular methods include markers that are water-soluble in nature, using heat-erasing pens and also chalks that can be easily washed away.

3. **Use your walking foot**

This shouldn't be a new idea to you at this stage of this book because this is what this book is all about. The walking foot essentially helps you achieve straight lines as you quilt, and it is a must have.

Awesome Tips For Stitching In-The-Ditch

1. Many quilters that uses machine are fond of rolling their basted quilt in order to prevent the bulk of their quilt from getting into the way as they stitch. The rolled part is often placed over their shoulder. This isn't good ergonomically. The ideal thing to do is rolling the part of the top you wish to get out of the way, then the excess should now be placed on your laps and not over your shoulder. With smaller quilts, this is very easy.

2. Endeavor to stitch very close to the seam, as close as you can get. This should be done on the side that doesn't have a seam allowance.

3. You should only stitch only where a seam is available. What this entails is that you have to think ahead as you press the top.

4. To start, one of the line of the in-the-ditch quilting should be stitched by the seam vertically. This should not be done in it. This should be done at the center of the quilt, either in the center or close to it. After that, the next line should be horizontally stitched in order to intersect the line you first stitched, near or inside the center of the quilt. This is very easy for quilts having borders and also having sashing too.

Helpful Hints For Quilting Design Motifs

1. As you quilt with the walking foot on your machine, you can start quilting anywhere provided the basic in-the-ditch stitching has been done and the quilt edge has been secured. If you wish, you can start with the border design.

2. As you stitch block designs, start by stitching the ones that are closer to the edge. You should develop your skill before you think of the blocks in the middle. The fabric bulk makes stitching in the middle difficult.

Tips On Handling Common Issues That Arises With Your Walking Foot

When working with your walking foot, you might encounter some problems, which as stated earlier might me unnoticeable, while still yet others might be costly. Without wasting much time, here are some of the very popular problems and how to fix them.

1. Puckering
2. Stitch length not adding up
3. Development of dog legs

1. Puckering

Quilters usually notice this when they push up their fabric against the needle. In doing so, when the needle pops out of the work, excess fabric gets pushed through, more than is required for the particular stitch.

Do you wonder why this happens? The reason why this happens could be because your hands are not properly position. This means that your hands are stationed past the needle that is pushing your material against the needle.

Another reason why quilters experience puckering could be that there is excessive quilt beneath the harp which is being forced up against the needle.

With that said, as you quilt, ensure that the quilt isn't forced up against the needle before you start and also during the sewing process.

You can avoid puckering in a couple of ways, and one of such is by having your left hand on top of the quilt, and as you do so, your fingers should form a V-shape right at the front of the needle with a space between the middle finger and the pointer finger too. Then you should have your right hand providing support for the quilt from under at the front. You can interchange your hands, and probably use the right hand instead of the left for providing the V-shape, depending on which hand works best for you.

Doing so makes the speed reduced, making it possible for you to be able to stitch just some inches before you can have a break and then remove your top hand (the one you formed a V-shape with) out of the needle's path.

This also brings great control as you sew, and also makes your stitching better. Even if this might seem like a lot of work to you, it is worth it as it provides more quality for your stitching.

Note that if your sewing tabletop is flat and large between your stomach and the needle, then there is no need placing your hand underneath to provide support since this table is helping you already with that job.

2. **Stitch length not adding up**
   This might come as an unpleasant surprise. The reason why such uneven stitch length occurs is because of using different speeds as you sew. When using the walking

foot, you are expected to work at an equal pace and slowly too.

So far, most quilters prefer using only two different types of speeds when quilting, and these are the stop and the flat out. Using the flat out speed usually tends to result in smaller stitches which are obvious.

Adjusting your sewing speeds to attain a new habit can take a long time. Nevertheless, if you are finding it hard, it is advisable to adjust and reduce your machine speed to half, or you can even reduce it further to be slower. This will make your quilt come out neatly and perfectly.

As you quilt, you can also encounter uneven stitches if a part of the walking foot comes in contact with a pin. To prevent this, it is very vital to remove any pin that stands in front of the foot or behind it.

Does your sewing machine come with a pressure dial? Then ensure to set it to match the actual height for the thickness of the fabric. This pressure dial raises up or drops down the presser foot when the foot is in use. If the material you are sewing is thin, then you should consider lowering the presser foot to ensure that the sole of the foot gets in contact with the fabrics. On the other hand, if the fabric you are sewing is thicker, you should consider lifting the presser foot a little higher to ensure that the fabric or quilt moves properly under the foot.

3. **Development Of Dog Legs**

Dog legs appear when your stitching jumps out of position. Dog legs appearing as you stitch could be a nightmare. Before you freak out, it is important to know some possible reasons while these dog legs appear.

- One of the reasons dog legs appear is when you move your hands on the top of the quilt with the machine still sewing. When the needle gets off the work with your hands removed from the quilt, you are giving the quilt the liberty to move in any direction it wants. This is more evident if the quilt hangs partly off the table giving room for the force of gravity to weigh it down.

- Another reason you may encounter dog legs is when you are using the function of needle up/needle down on the machine. You remove your foot from the pedal and the needle still has to move back into the work. As you do so, you might think that the machine will cease to function as you remove your foot from the pedal. With this assumption, you go ahead and remove your hands from the quilt just immediately before the needle gets fixed in the work.

- Dog legs can also appear if you don't hold the quilt very tightly when you sew the first stitch or even the last stitch. This can be fixed by pushing down on the back of your hand then systematically move the skin in a controlled manner. You can hold down on the skin in a tough way or in a gentle manner and still move the skin backward and forward. This has to be done to the quilt as you are making the first stitch and also when making the last stitch before you put your sewing machine to a stop. You just push it down in a controlled manner, but you still give the feed dogs the allowance needed to move the quilt underneath the needle.

- Using a smaller stitch length might become necessary when you sew a curve. It has been observed that the more the stitches, the smoother the curve becomes. If you decide to go for a large stitch as at when sewing a curve, it might get off the line. The walking foot is capable of handling gentle curves, however, you will have to turn the quilt earlier than you think is the right time to do so.

More Tips On Using The Walking Foot Perfectly

1. Ensure that you use a stitch length which is a bit longer in order to contain the bulk when using a batting that is thicker. As a general rule, you might consider matching or complementing the stitch length of your free motion work when the element sizes are almost the same.

2. Ensure that you perfect the art of putting on the walking foot. The bar should go over the top or around the needle nut. When you correctly mount the walking foot, several errors are avoided.

3. An open toe foot is highly recommended because it allows you to have a better view of the ditch or marked line as you sew.

4. It has been stated before, and I will still say it again: don't go too fast with your walking foot. Going too

fast will make the fabric unable to move as smoothly as it should.

5. Ensure that most of the quilt is supported on your laps or the table top when you quilt. This is because it can be difficult for your feed dogs to smoothly move the quilt if it hangs over the edges.

6. Endeavor to increase your stitch length just a little bit when quilting with your walking foot. For instance, you can increase it to 3 if the normal length you use is 2.5.

7. You can make use of a guide bar that is attached to your walking foot as an alternative to marking out the whole top.

8. If it happens that you will cross over stitching, you should try putting a bit tension on the top of the quilt when you get very close to the stitch line, this will help get rid of tucks.

9. To get a more flat quilt, one which will be easier to quilt, press the seams open.

10. Practice on a sample block. If you aren't yet sure of how to quilt a particular space, it is advisable to practice. You may decide to keep quilt sandwiches close to your machine, preferably a square quilt of about 10″. Not only if you aren't sure of how to quilt should this be done. Even if you are sure of what to quilt, it will be very beneficial if you practice for some minutes before you begin quilting.

11. Baste your quilt, preferably with a spray baste.

12. Planning is important. If you are not very sure of the design, you can try drawing it out on an acetate sheet or plastic notebook divider. With this done, put the drawing over your quilt top, then assess your design. If it looks great, you should begin quilting. If you don't like the design, you should try drawing a different design and compare.

13.   Practice, they say makes perfect. This isn't just a motivational talk. It is true and should also be applied to quilting. As you practice more often, you tend to know the ups and downs as you quilt and also get to know your walking foot better. This improves your confidence and makes your quilting better. With constant practice, the stitches gets neater, the corners appear tighter, the rows looks straighter, and everything starts becoming perfect.

Chapter IV

Now You Can Begin Quilting

How To Quilt With The Walking Foot

Congratulations, you are about to walk into the process of using your walking foot for quilting! When you are new to quilting, you might get intimidated by many things, and one of them is sitting down then start quilting a top that you have already pieced. However, this shouldn't be so.

Quilting with the walking foot is one of the easiest ways to quilt because of the great assistance the walking foot provides.

What You Will Need To Start Quilting With Your Walking Foot

To start quilting with the walking foot, you will need the following materials:

Some Materials Needed For Quilting

- Quilt top that has been pieced.
- Quilting thread
- Masking tape (painter's tape).
- Mat for cutting
- Your walking foot
- Your sewing machine
- Spray baste
- Batting (it is advisable to use 3-4" bigger in both directions than your walking foot).
- Iron
- Backing fabric (this should be 3-4" larger in both directions than your batting).
- Rotary cutter
- Gloves for quilting (this is highly recommended for larger quilts)

Useful Tips For The Type Of Supplies To Use

Before we move further, I'll like to point out some helpful tips to consider as you choose supplies.

1. To achieve smooth stitching, it is advisable to use top-quality cotton threads of 50 weight in your bobbin, regardless of the weight on the top.

2. To achieve much more straighter stitches, it is greatly recommended to use needles that have a sharp point.

3. Heavier threads (about 30-weight) can be used on the machine tops if the ideal needles and battings are used.

4. If you are using heavier threads like the 30 weight threads, Endeavour to use needles with a sharp point and

also a very large eye. You can use the size 16 top-stitching needle as this allows threads that are heavier to pass through.

5. It is recommended to use 50 weight threads and about ten (10) stitches for one inch if you do stitching in the ditch. This might seem a bit much longer than what is required for normal piecing, however, the walking foot has been proven to work in a smoother manner when this long stitch length is used.

Step-By-Step Instructions To Quilt Using Your Walking Foot

The First Step:

You Should Baste Your Quilt.

Start by bringing together your quilt sandwich. Normally, this should be done on a surface that is smooth, such as wood/tile floors. This surface should also be larger than your quilt back. You should use your tape to hold the quilt back on this smooth surface with the sight side facing down. This is to ensure that it doesn't shift.

You might not have a surface that is large enough. If that is the case, use the space you have and the same process. However, ensure that you work in sections over your quilt on the surface you have, probably a tabletop. Remember that working with a spray baste needs ventilation. Hence, ensure that the space you are using is well ventilated, or you can do it outside.

The next thing to do is to lay your batting on top of the backing, then you should start smoothing from the middle, then outwards. As you do so, ensure that your batting doesn't have any folds, puckers or creases.

After you have made sure everything is smooth, at a time, raise up one part of the batting, and the with the use of your spay baste, secure in place. Don't forget to smoothen right from the middle outwards.

Now, you should place your quilt top in a center position, with the right side upwards on your batting. You should again raise sections in order to spray baste the top of the batting, and remember to work from the middle to the outer part.

As soon as you have spayed all down, you should now carefully remove the tape and remove your quilt from the surface used for basting, then carefully transfer it to your board for ironing.

Using a dry iron, ensure that the whole quilt is lightly pressed now that you have successfully spray basted. Doing this ensures that everything becomes more secure and smoother before you move on to quilting.

SPECIAL NOTE: Even though I have talked about preparing your quilting top, there are other strategies that will help you.

1. It is advisable to limit the first machine-quilted project you embark on to a much smaller size. This makes it very easy for you to handle the bulk.
2. Ensure that you press properly as you piece your quilt. This is to ensure that all the seams are properly pressed in constant directions. As you press, remember that is will be beneficial for you to do a final touch-up pressing before you start quilting.

3. If the edge of your quilt top comes with plenty of seams, you may want to consider stitching all around the edge, probably at 1/8" to ¼" on the inside. This will help preventing the seams from coming undone. Nevertheless, if the borders of the quilt are unpieced with corner blocks, you might want to consider stitching at ½" over the corner block seams.

The Second Step:

Your walking foot should be attached.

Your machine should now be prepared for quilting with your working foot. You should attach the walking foot. If you don't know how to attach the walking foot, please refer to the part of this book where I talked about attaching your walking foot. Attaching the walking foot might seem complicated at first, but it is really simply. It involves mounting it on your presser foot, sliding it so it sits around the needle bar, then possibly tightening it with a lever, clip or screw, depending on your sewing machine.

The Third Step:

Get Your Stitch Setup.

The next thing to do after successfully attaching your walking foot is to select and allow the walking foot you are using to be recognized if your machine allows it.

Choose a running stitch, and with the help of your multifunction knobs, adjust the stitch length and width. If you change the length of your stitch, your individual stitches will be adjusted in length. However, as you look, you will be able to see the distance between the changes in waves. If you adjust the width of your stitch, the depth of the waves will be altered.

The Fourth Step:

Begin Stitching.

This is it! Pick a point to begin quilting. While some loves to begin from the middle, others prefer starting from an end to the next end. If you are not sure which one to try, it is a great advice to practice on a separate piece, not your main quilt. As you do so, whichever, point you later select, you should ensure that your stitching is consistent.

Begin stitching off the edge of your quilt top, then stitch from one of the edge to the other. As you stitch from edge to edge, there is no need worrying about getting any thread buried.

As you reach the opposite side of your quilt, stitch your quilt top edges off, then cut the threads. With this done, go back to the beginning end of your quilt to start the next row.

This stitch should be repeated with the current settings you used in regular space per the size of your block. What this entails is that if your quilt features blocks of 8″, you have to repeat the stitching rows at an interval of 8″ across the quilt.

SPECIAL NOTE: To achieve better stitching, these hints will help:

1. Prepare a stitching sample before you start quilting. You might want to make tension adjustments, and this is really necessary if you are using the 30 weight threads.

2. Don't be scared to play around and experiment with the tension of your machine. When using a 30 weight thread, it is very likely that the top tension will be loosen. You can try half steps. If you notice that loosening the tension isn't working, you may consider tightening it a bit.

3. If nice stitches are something you find hard to achieve using heavier threads, you should rethread your machine. It is likely that you might not have made it properly seated in the tension mechanism.

4. Don't forget to always bring the bobbin thread up when you begin stitching. Both threads should be placed beneath the walking foot, then hold them as you slowly begin to stitch.

5. For the 50-weight thread to be secured, the length of your stitch should be reduced and you should stitch about 1/8″ to ¼″ at the start and also at the end of your quilting. Such securing stitch is usually used when the stitching ends at the quilt top edge. Alternatively, the securing stitches could be hidden near a crossing seam.

6. Note that a securing stitch cannot be used with threads that are heavier (like the 30-weight), and this is because the stitching that is short-length reveals too much. The thing to do here is to leave like 4″ lengths of the top and the bottom threads at the start and also at the end of your stitching. These ends of the thread are taken to the back of your quilt, then they are knotted off. The tails now get buried between the layers of the quilt, just like it is done when you hand quilt.

7. You should practice your sewing at a moderate and smooth speed. Desist from sewing fast, and also don't engage in rough starts and stops.

The Fifth Step:

Adjust The Settings Of Your Quilt.

Go back to the screen of your machine. Now, change the length of your stitch. You can also change the width. Whichever one you change, it will assist you in developing texture all over your quilt.

The Sixth Step:

Repeat The Stitching.

The stitching process, right from step four and step five should be repeated. This entails stitching from one end of your quilt to the other end of your quilt at a regular interval. You should also change your wave pattern for each full pass you complete across your quilt.

The Seventh Step:

Wrapping It All Up.

As soon as you have successfully quilted in the density you desire, you should start finishing it up. At this point, your quilt should be squared, and you should trim away all the excess batting and backing fabric. Bind, then label as you wish.

That is it! Not as difficult as you thought, isn't it? Take a look at your finished project. I am sure you are proud of it!

What To Do From Here

Congratulations, you have come to the end of this book on walking foot quilting for beginners! It is one thing to know about the walking foot, and it is something else to practice using it just once. However, if you want to be a professional, if you want to fast track your success from beginner to pro, you should practice, practice, and practice! Yes, keep practicing because practice, they say, makes perfect.

Don't forget to always use this book as a reference or guide as you begin your journey into the quilting world.

If you find this book helpful, please Endeavour to drop a review on the Amazon product page as this will help me a lot. Thank you!

Printed in Great Britain
by Amazon